UNSUNG HEROES OF
SCIENCE

by Todd Kortemeier

STORY LIBRARY

www.12StoryLibrary.com

Copyright © 2017 by Peterson Publishing Company, North Mankato, MN 56003. All rights reserved. No part of this book may be reproduced or utilized in any form or by any means without written permission from the publisher.

12-Story Library is an imprint of Peterson Publishing Company and Press Room Editions.

Produced for 12-Story Library by Red Line Editorial

Photographs ©: Bettmann/Corbis, cover, 1, 27; Dorling Kindersley/Thinkstock, 4, 28; Jonathan Blair/ Corbis, 5; Colin McPherson/Corbis, 6; Anthony Devlin/PA Wire URN:24476906/AP Images, 7; Jacob Harris/AP Images, 8; AP Images, 10, 23, 26; Ann Rosener/FSA/OWI Collection/Library of Congress, 11; Anest/iStockphoto, 12; AS400 DB/Bettmann/Corbis, 13; Universal History Archive/UIG/Getty Images, 14, 29; Alfred A. Hart/Library of Congress, 16; Malekas85/iStockphoto, 17; Solodov Alexey/ Shutterstock Images, 19; Detroit Publishing Company/Library of Congress, 18, 20; Corbis, 22; Public Domain, 24; proxyminder/istockphoto, 25

Library of Congress Cataloging-in-Publication Data

Names: Kortemeier, Todd, 1986- author.
Title: Unsung heroes of science / by Todd Kortemeier.
Description: North Mankato, MN : 12-Story Library, [2017] | Series: Unsung
   heroes | Audience: Grades 4 to 6. | Includes bibliographical references
   and index.
Identifiers: LCCN 2016002371 (print) | LCCN 2016008299 (ebook) | ISBN
   9781632353092 (library bound : alk. paper) | ISBN 9781632353597 (pbk. :
   alk. paper) | ISBN 9781621434733 (hosted ebook)
Subjects: LCSH: Scientists--Biography--Juvenile literature. |
   Science--History--Juvenile literature.
Classification: LCC T39 .K677 2016 (print) | LCC T39 (ebook) | DDC
   509.22--dc23
LC record available at http://lccn.loc.gov/2016002371

Printed in the United States of America
Mankato, MN
May, 2016

Access free, up-to-date content on this topic plus a full digital version of this book. Scan the QR code on page 31 or use your school's login at 12StoryLibrary.com.

Table of Contents

Mary Anning Hunts for Fossils

Mary Anning's life was filled with great discoveries. Many were made in her home country of England. England's capital, London, was considered a center of scientific thought during the 1800s. But Anning lived in tiny Lyme Regis, far removed from London. And women were not thought of as equal participants in making scientific history.

Anning was born in 1799 on the southern coast of England. She spent much of her childhood walking the nearby cliffs. Her family was poor. But the area was rich in dinosaur fossils. The Anning family collected and sold fossils to support themselves. Finding fossils was dangerous work. The cliffs were slippery and unstable. Anning showed a good eye for finding fossils from a young age.

By the 1820s, Anning had taken over running the family business. Most of her amazing finds were sold to museums and personal collections. But she did not get credit for most of the fossils she found. Because she was a woman and had no educational background, the scientific community dismissed her.

Anning collected and sold fossils.

Anning discovered the first full Ichthyosaurus fossil, similar to this one.

Among Anning's notable finds were full skeletons of Ichthyosaurus and Plesiosaurus. These were the first known complete examples ever found. Both were swimming dinosaurs. But even these discoveries earned Anning only limited recognition. She was

disappointed that she didn't have a bigger role in science.

Time has recognized Anning's achievements. In 2010, the Royal Society of London named her one of the top ten British women in scientific history.

12

Anning's age when she found the Ichthyosaurus fossil.

- Anning was born in 1799.
- The Anning family collected and sold fossils.
- Anning found the first known full skeletons of two dinosaurs, Ichthyosaurus and Plesiosaurus.
- In 2010, Anning was named one of the most influential female British scientists.

ANNING'S NAME LIVES ON

Anning found the Ichthyosaurus skeleton in approximately 1811. Nearly 200 years later, in 2008, a new species was discovered. It was given a fitting name, *Ichthyosaurus anningae*, in her honor.

Jocelyn Bell Burnell Discovers Pulsars

Jocelyn Bell Burnell liked to say she "started by failing." Growing up in Northern Ireland, she failed a major exam at age 11. In the middle of the twentieth century, most of the world did not value women's education. But Burnell's family did. They sent her to boarding school to focus on her studies. Burnell enjoyed learning. Astronomy was her favorite subject.

Burnell continued her studies through college. She faced discrimination from male students. Some of them taunted her when she simply walked into the classroom. She earned a PhD from Cambridge University.

As a PhD student, Burnell worked on a team that was researching radio waves in space. Detecting these waves required a huge telescope. It was made up of thousands of poles and wires. Burnell assisted in its construction. When the telescope received a signal, it printed it out on a piece of paper. Burnell reviewed all of these signals.

In November 1967, Burnell saw an odd signal. She thought it might be a mistake. But she noticed it kept appearing. At first, the team thought it could be an alien signal. It turned out not to be quite that exciting. But in astronomical history, it was incredible. The signal was the mark of a pulsar. A pulsar is a star that spins

Jocelyn Bell Burnell

24
Age of Burnell when she discovered pulsars.

- Burnell was interested in astronomy from an early age.
- She studied physics and then pursued her PhD at Cambridge University.
- Her research led to the discovery of pulsars.
- Two of her male colleagues were awarded the Nobel Prize, but she was not.

THINK ABOUT IT

Bell did not receive the Nobel Prize even though she was a key part of the discovery. Have you ever not gotten credit you felt you deserved? How did you handle it?

Burnell continued her amazing career in science. She never won the Nobel Prize but earned many other scientific awards. As of 2016, she worked as a professor in the United Kingdom.

very quickly. Nobody knew that they existed.

In the coming years, scientists used Burnell's research to learn more about pulsars. In 1974, two advisors at Cambridge won the Nobel Prize for the discovery. Burnell was excluded. She believed the advisors were chosen because they were men. The committee probably assumed they had made the discovery. Some in the scientific community argued for Burnell to be recognized, but she never was.

Burnell was honored with the Prudential Woman of the Year award in 2015.

3

Marie Daly Earns Chemistry PhD

Marie Daly got many things from her father. One was her love of chemistry. Another was his belief in the importance of education. Daly's father had to drop out of college because he didn't have enough money. So he expected that Daly would get her degree. For a black

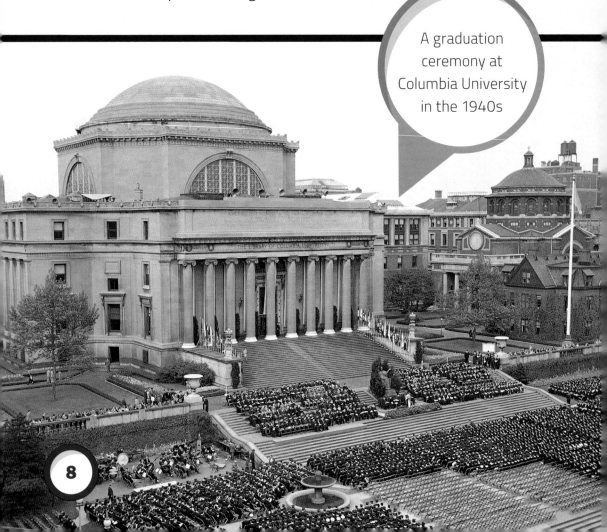

A graduation ceremony at Columbia University in the 1940s

woman in the 1930s, that was still quite rare.

Daly attended Queens College near her home in New York City. She was an excellent chemistry student and graduated in 1942. She then worked part time in a lab at the college. At the same time, she worked on her master's degree at New York University. She went on to Columbia University to pursue her PhD. Normally, she might not have been able to get in. But the United States was fighting World War II. A lot of men were off fighting the war. That opened up more opportunities for women.

Daly's research focused on how the body digests food. She received her PhD in chemistry in 1947, just three years after she started. She was the first black woman in the United States to earn this degree. After school, Daly began her career in medical research. Her work showed a link between diet and clogged arteries. This gave people

1

Number of years it took for Daly to finish her master's degree.

- Daly grew up wanting to study chemistry.
- She earned a bachelor's degree in chemistry and then a master's.
- She earned her PhD in three years, becoming the first black woman to ever earn one in the United States.
- She discovered a link between eating certain foods and having clogged arteries.

more information on how their food choices affected their health. Daly's later research studied the effects of smoking on a person's lungs.

In 1988, Daly formed a program to help minority science students. She created a scholarship at Queens College in her father's name. It helped make sure minorities had an equal chance at finishing their degrees.

Charles Drew Makes Blood Banks Possible

The man who invented the blood bank couldn't even donate to it because of the color of his skin. Charles Drew did not let that stop him. He saved thousands of lives with his research on blood transfusions. But because of racist attitudes toward black people, Drew's blood was not accepted at blood banks during his lifetime.

As a young man, Drew did not have an interest in medicine. In high school, he was a great athlete, which opened many doors for him. In 1922, Drew received a sports scholarship to attend Amherst College. Drew was one of only 13 black students at the college. His biology professor encouraged him to pursue a medical career. Drew decided to follow the advice. But the field was not common for black people at the time.

Drew did not have many options for medical school. Schools were divided by race. The best ones let in only a few black students each year. So Drew got his medical degree in Montreal, Canada, at McGill University. Drew was one of the top students at McGill. But after he graduated, he struggled

Charles Drew

1,320

Amount of plasma, in gallons (5,000 L), shipped overseas by Drew's donation program in less than six months.

- Drew became interested in medicine in college.
- He had trouble being admitted to schools and finding a job because he was a black man.
- Drew understood the value of blood transfusion.
- He developed a system for storing blood plasma that saved lives.

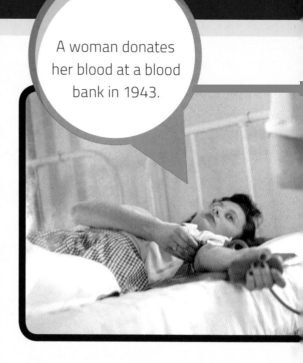

A woman donates her blood at a blood bank in 1943.

to find a job at a hospital. Many did not hire black people. Some patients had racist views and did not want black doctors.

Drew was interested in the process of exchanging blood, called transfusion. This field was becoming important. In 1939, World War II began in Europe. By 1941, the United States had entered the conflict. Blood was needed for injured soldiers. More useful than blood was plasma. Plasma is a liquid that carries blood cells through the body. It can be used in place of blood and for any blood type. This made it helpful in emergencies. But it was hard to keep plasma fresh and usable.

Drew's research made it possible to ship plasma overseas. It also made it possible to store it for later use. This led to the first blood banks. Eventually, blood donations became accepted from all races. Countless lives have been saved thanks to Drew's work.

Drew died in a car accident in 1950. But in an attempt to save his life, he received a blood transfusion—from a white-only hospital.

Carlos Juan Finlay Finds the Cause of Yellow Fever

In the late 1800s, yellow fever was spreading throughout Central America. Dr. Carlos Juan Finlay was an expert on this deadly disease. The Cuban government chose him to find out its cause. Finlay spent two years studying the disease. In 1881, he presented his findings.

Finlay believed mosquitoes carried the disease. He observed that there was a certain species usually found in homes affected by yellow fever. The peak season for the disease lined up with mosquito season. He believed that when infected mosquitoes stung people, the disease spread. But when Finlay spoke about his findings, nobody believed him. Some scientists laughed at him. He worked to convince them, but it took decades.

It wasn't until 1900 that Finlay finally found a believer. A group of Americans came to Cuba to study the disease. The group was led by US Army doctor Walter Reed. Reed's team came specifically to test Finlay's mosquito theory. They were able to confirm his findings.

Then they set out to destroy the mosquito population. The capital of Havana became free of

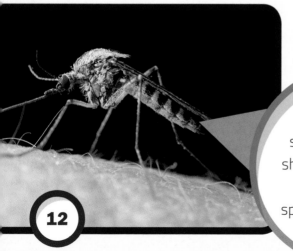

At first, other scientists did not share Finlay's belief that mosquitos spread yellow fever.

100,000

Estimated number of yellow fever deaths in Cuba from 1854 through 1898.

- Finlay was a Cuban-born doctor who researched yellow fever.
- He discovered a link between the disease and bites from mosquitoes.
- Finlay's research was not taken seriously.
- In 1900, a team of US doctors confirmed Finlay's results.
- Yellow fever was eliminated from Cuba.

A GLOBAL CITIZEN

Finlay had a very diverse background. His father was Scottish, and his mother was French. He was born in Cuba but went to school in France and the United States. Finlay spoke French, German, English, and Spanish. He could also read Latin.

yellow fever for the first time in 150 years. Removing the threat saved thousands of lives. And it made the area more habitable.

The US Army's main medical center would later be named for Reed. He also would become known as the one to link mosquitoes and yellow fever. But it was Finlay's research that made it possible. A statue of Finlay was put up in Cuba after his death in 1915. It was featured on a stamp in 1965.

Finlay's discovery saved lives.

Rosalind Franklin Discovers the Structure of DNA

The 1950s were a challenging time to be a female scientist. Many people during this time did not think women should study science. Rosalind Franklin was interested in science from a young age. But it was hard to find a school that had science programs for girls in London, where she lived. Even her father was not supportive. He didn't believe women should get a higher education. But she did it anyway.

Franklin went to the University of Cambridge, one of the best schools in the world. She later got her PhD there as well. Franklin worked in Paris for a time.

Franklin wanted to discover the structure of DNA.

Then she returned to Cambridge to work in a research lab. Her work was primarily on the structure of DNA. DNA is a molecule in all living things. It carries genetic information. Discovering its structure was a big goal in science at the time.

Franklin took a picture that cracked the DNA code. She spent many hours with an x-ray machine trying to get a photo of DNA structure. She took one photo called Photograph 51 that would later become world famous. The photo showed DNA in an X shape. Franklin didn't know at the time that it revealed the structure of DNA.

Franklin's photo led James Watson and Francis Crick to the discovery first. Franklin came very close to solving it herself. But Watson and Crick beat her to publication. In 1962, it won them the Nobel Prize. But Franklin did not live to see it. She died of cancer at the age of 37. Although Franklin was not honored with a Nobel Prize, her work was essential to understanding DNA.

15

Franklin's age when she decided to become a scientist.

- Franklin was interested in chemistry from an early age.
- She attended the University of Cambridge.
- She studied x-rays of DNA to determine its structure.
- One of her photographs was essential to the discovery of the structure of DNA.

THINK ABOUT IT

Franklin had a hard time just finding a school to get her education. Is this still true today? What are some roadblocks today to women and minorities getting equal opportunities?

Lue Gim Gong Saves Florida's Citrus Industry

Growing up in China in the mid-1800s, Lue Gim Gong dreamed of the United States. Lue begged his parents to let him move there. Even though Lue was still a teenager, his parents let him go. Lue traveled with his uncle to San Francisco, California. Lue eventually worked his way across the country to Massachusetts. There, he got a job at a shoe factory.

There was plenty of work for Chinese immigrants in the United States. They worked for low wages, so many employers wanted to hire them. This made white workers angry. Many people wanted the Chinese workers out of Massachusetts.

Lue joined a church. The members helped him learn English. He met Fanny Burlingame. She offered him a job on her farm and a place to live. Lue's parents had been farmers in China. Lue and Burlingame became very close. She later adopted him as her son.

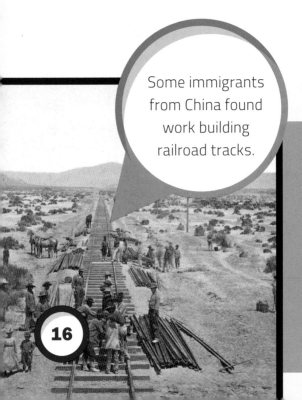

Some immigrants from China found work building railroad tracks.

LUE'S OTHER FRUITS

Lue was skilled with other plants as well. He was able to make fruits that ripened earlier. He bred grapefruits, apples, cherries, and peaches. The early-ripening peach meant that people could make peach pies earlier, in time for Thanksgiving.

200 million

Approximate number of crates of oranges currently produced in Florida each year.

- Lue Gim Gong was born in China but moved to the United States as a boy.
- He got a job working on a farm in Massachusetts.
- Lue moved to Florida, where he became interested in citrus fruits.
- He bred a species of orange that could survive frost.
- This species, sold today as a Valencia orange, made Florida's citrus industry more profitable.

Lue made a lasting impact on the citrus industry.

Lue was talented at tending to the plants. But he suffered from ill health made worse by the winter. Burlingame recommended that he move to Florida, where she owned an orchard. In Florida, Lue learned all about growing oranges and other fruits. During the winter of 1894 and 1895, the weather in Florida was harsh. Almost the entire orchard crop was ruined. Lue worked on breeding an orange that could survive harsher winters.

Lue's experiments took a long time to perfect. Another harsh winter in 1904 wiped out most of the crop. But by 1909, Lue had made an orange that resisted frost. It was also sweeter. And it ripened earlier so it avoided the worst of winter. People started to call Lue "The Citrus Wizard." His work saved one of Florida's most important industries.

Lue never profited much from his discovery. A company with which he was in business sold his orange seeds without paying him for them. During Lue's lifetime, his orange was simply called the "Lue Gim Gong." Today, it is called the Valencia orange.

Ernest E. Just Changes How We Look at Cells

Ernest E. Just had to leave home to get his chance at an education. He was born in South Carolina in 1883. Educational opportunities for black men during this time were few. At just 17 years old, he left to study in Vermont. He'd earned a scholarship to a boarding school. He was the only black student there. He then went to Dartmouth College. He was a double major in history and biology.

Marine biology became the focus of Just's career. Despite having been a good student, he found few opportunities to teach. He took one of only two open jobs at Howard College. Howard was traditionally a school for only black people.

Just first taught English. Within two years, he was teaching biology.

Just was interested in marine biology and zoology. But there were very few black zoologists. Just traveled frequently to the Woods Hole Institute in Massachusetts. It was one of the best marine biology labs in the world. But he still experienced discrimination. He took his family along to Woods Hole one summer. They were the targets of threats and offensive language from some people. Just was very discouraged. He began to seek opportunities in Europe, where racism was less widespread in some areas.

Just studied history and biology at Dartmouth College.

Just also faced challenges to his theories. He focused his research on cells. He studied the cells of marine animals. Other scientists believed that genes influenced development. Just argued that cells were like a scaled-down version of the living being itself. The way the cell developed determined how the whole creature developed.

Just struggled to advance these views during his lifetime. But in recent years, his contribution to the understanding of cells has been recognized. He greatly influenced how biologists analyze living systems today.

70
Number of papers Just published in his career, most of which were not widely known until the 1980s.

- Just was a strong student who struggled to find work because of racist attitudes of the time.
- Just taught at Howard College and researched marine biology.
- In studying the cells of marine mammals, he believed cells were the key to an animal's development.
- Just's contributions were largely ignored until after his death.

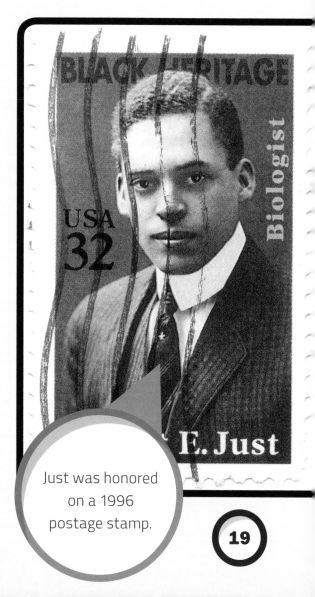

Just was honored on a 1996 postage stamp.

Henrietta Swan Leavitt Calculates the Universe

Henrietta Swan Leavitt's education could match that of any male astronomer. But for a woman in the late 1800s, that didn't matter. Leavitt had to start out at the very bottom. Fortunately for the future of astronomy, she didn't stay there.

Leavitt studied many different subjects at Radcliffe College. But astronomy interested her the most. She got a job at the Harvard College Observatory in 1893. There, women were trusted with only the most basic of tasks. Leavitt classified stars according to their brightness.

Leavitt worked at Harvard College Observatory.

She worked with other educated women doing the same work.

Classifying the stars was more like organizing than actual study. But Leavitt took it seriously. Most of her work was with variable stars. These are stars with brightness that changes over a period of time. They are important because a star's brightness can be used to tell how far away it is. But it can be difficult to tell if a dim star is far away or just not very bright.

It was Leavitt who solved this mystery. She concentrated on a group of variable stars. Since they were all found in the same area, she determined that they must be similar distances from Earth. She recorded their maximum brightness. She also recorded how long it took for a star to go dim, then back to bright. She discovered brighter stars took longer. So if she could get the actual distance for one of these stars, she could figure out what brightness

2,400
Number of stars Leavitt discovered, half of all that were known at the time.

- Leavitt was interested in astronomy and began working at the Harvard College Observatory.
- While classifying stars by brightness, Leavitt came up with a way to determine their distance from Earth.
- This model was used in future astronomical discoveries.

equaled what distance. The distance of one star was determined a couple of years later. Leavitt's model was used in many future discoveries.

Because of her gender, Leavitt was prevented from having a bigger career in science. She continued to work at the observatory until she died in 1921. She is remembered as a brilliant mind in the observatory's history.

Lise Meitner Helps Discover Nuclear Fission

Lise Meitner faced many challenges as a scientist in Austria. It was the early 1900s, and few opportunities were open to her. She earned a PhD in physics in 1905. But even that did not open many doors. The only work she could get was as a schoolteacher. So she left Austria and went to Berlin, Germany.

There, Meitner met Otto Hahn. She and Hahn became friends and worked together. Nuclear physics was a growing area of study. This is where Meitner and Hahn focused their energies in the 1930s. A nuclear reaction, resulting in nuclear fission, had a lot of potential uses.

MEITNER'S ELEMENT

Meitner never got her name on a Nobel Prize. But her name does live on in science history. German scientists discovered a new element in 1982. They called it *meitnerium* in her honor.

Meitner was a pioneer in nuclear fission.

It was an energy source. And it had possible use as a weapon. But fission had yet to be created.

Hahn and Meitner had made a lot of progress in their research. But soon they faced a roadblock. In 1938, the Nazis were driving Jewish people out of Germany. World War II was on the horizon. Meitner was part Jewish. She had to leave Berlin. She ended up in Sweden but stayed in touch with Hahn. He and another scientist made a big discovery later that year. They had produced another element in a nuclear reaction. They reported this to Meitner, who calculated that it was the proof of nuclear fission that they had hoped for.

The discovery of nuclear fission led to the Manhattan Project in the United States. That work ultimately created the atomic bombs that were dropped on Japan. Meitner and her associates did not do any of that research. But, in 1944, Hahn won the Nobel Prize for the discovery of nuclear fission. Meitner's role in the discovery was not recognized at the time. She continued to do nuclear research for the rest of her career.

1966

Year Meitner was awarded the Fermi Prize for achievement in energy development.

- Meitner earned her PhD in physics.
- She went to work with Otto Hahn on nuclear energy.
- Meitner confirmed Hahn had produced nuclear fission, making future nuclear research possible.

Meitner was greeted by press on a trip to the United States in 1946.

Charles Henry Turner Discovers Amazing Insect Facts

After the Civil War, slavery was illegal throughout the United States. But formerly enslaved people still faced challenges. Charles Henry Turner was born in 1867, two years after the war ended. His mother was a former slave. Turner's parents encouraged him to get an education.

Turner graduated at the top of his high school class. He studied biology in college and earned a master's degree. He then became the first black man to receive a PhD from the University of Chicago.

Turner became an authority on animal behavior. He had published more than 30 papers. But he still could not find a teaching position at the college level. He spent his career teaching at various high schools while continuing his research. Turner studied a wide variety of animals and insects.

Some of Turner's most important work was with honeybees. He was able to prove that bees could see in color. This helped scientists understand what kinds of flowers bees are attracted to. He also was able to

Turner worked hard on his research and published many papers.

THINK ABOUT IT

Turner had a unique way of observing animal behavior that hadn't been done before. What other qualities or skills do you think make a good scientist?

70

Number of academic papers Turner published, making him one of the most published scientists ever.

- Turner was the first black person to receive a PhD from the University of Chicago.
- He did research on animal behavior, especially the behavior of honeybees.
- His discoveries changed how scientists observed animal behavior.

attract bees with food at certain times of the day. This demonstrated that bees could in some way understand time. Before Turner's discovery, nobody knew insects had these capabilities.

But Turner's research was forgotten for years. Later publications on the same discoveries did not credit Turner at all. But his methods for observing animal behavior became widely followed. Scientists today use Turner's comparative model of observation. This relies on comparing experiments with different variables, such as the age of the animal.

Turner also became active in the civil rights movement. He helped organize social services for black people in Saint Louis, Missouri. He died at the age of 55, shortly after retiring from teaching. There are several schools around Saint Louis named for him.

Turner studied honeybees and other insects.

Chien-Shiung Wu Pioneers Nuclear Research

The "First Lady of Physics" took an unlikely path to get this title. Chien-Shiung Wu was born in a small town in China in 1912. Her parents believed in women's education. They even started a school for that purpose. Wu graduated at the top of her class. She then studied physics at college. But there were not many opportunities in China for a female physicist. She decided to come to the United States.

Wu earned her physics PhD in 1940. She was such a good student that she was asked to work on a special project. It was the Manhattan Project at Columbia University. The purpose of the Manhattan Project was to create an atomic bomb. Wu developed a way to use the element uranium as nuclear fuel. Her method was able to produce a lot of uranium. This was very important to the success of the project.

Wu remained as a researcher at Columbia for her whole career. In 1956, she made her most notable discovery. She and a team of researchers disproved a law of

Wu (front right) received an honorary degree from Harvard University in 1974.

physics. It was called the Parity Law. It held that objects that were opposites behaved in opposite ways. Wu proved that this was not always true. As nuclear material decays, it gives off particles. Wu found that these particles sometimes fly off in one direction, not in opposite ones.

At the time, Wu's discovery was thought to be one of the most important in nuclear physics. In 1957, it earned a Nobel Prize, but not for Wu. Two of her male associates won it. Wu's contribution

Wu in a laboratory at Columbia University in 1958

was never noted. She won several lesser awards, but never the Nobel. Many believed it was because she was a woman. She became an advocate for women to enter the sciences.

1

Number of Chinese Americans working on the Manhattan Project. Wu was the only one.

- Wu was born in China and studied physics.
- She helped enrich uranium to use as nuclear fuel for the Manhattan Project.
- She disproved a law of physics, which earned her male colleagues the Nobel Prize.

LEAVING CHINA BEHIND

Wu left China in 1936. In 1937, Japan invaded. World War II broke out soon afterward. Because of the tension, Wu was unable to return to China to see her family. It was not until 1973 that she was able to go back to visit. She lived the rest of her life in the United States.

Fact Sheet

- Today, women earn about 57 percent of bachelor's degrees in the United States. Women also earn roughly half of all science and engineering degrees. The programs with the lowest female participation are engineering, computer science, and physics. But in most areas, the number of bachelor's degrees awarded to women in these subjects has been rising since 1993.

- The participation of minorities in science programs is on the rise. Minorities are less likely to graduate from high school and go on to college than white people. Most of the degrees that are earned by minorities are not in science or engineering. But some programs are on the rise, such as computer science and bioscience.

- In 1849, Elizabeth Blackwell became the first woman to earn a medical degree. She later became the first American woman doctor. In 1873, Ellen Swallow Richards became the first woman admitted to the highly-regarded Massachusetts Institute of Technology (MIT). She earned a chemistry degree and became the country's first working female chemist.

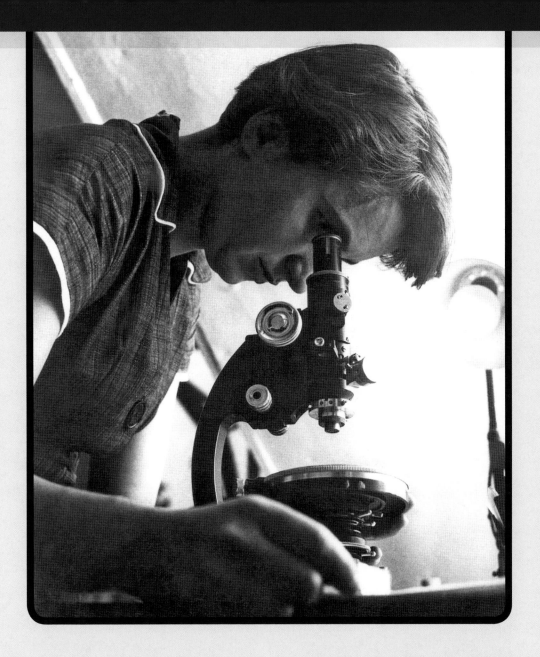

- In 1968, Luis Walter Alvarez became the first Hispanic person to be awarded the Nobel Prize for Physics.

- It wasn't until 1983 that the first black person flew in space. Guion Bluford flew on the space shuttle.

Glossary

astronomy
The study of the universe beyond Earth.

biology
The science of living things.

chemistry
The science of the composition of substances.

fission
The splitting of the nucleus, resulting in the release of atomic energy.

fossil
A remnant or impression of a once-living creature, such as a footprint or a piece of bone.

molecule
A very small unit of any compound.

nuclear
Refers to the nucleus, or center, of an atom; generally refers to the science of atomic weapons or energy.

observatory
A building that houses the equipment needed to study space and the sky.

PhD
An advanced degree, sometimes called a doctorate.

physics
The science of motion, force, and energy.

zoology
The science of studying animals.

For More Information

Books

Di Domenico, Kelly. *Women Scientists Who Changed the World.* New York: Rosen Publishing, 2011.

Jackson, Donna M. *Extreme Scientists.* Boston: Houghton Mifflin, 2014.

Richard, Orlin. *12 Scientists Who Changed the World.* Mankato, MN: Peterson Publishing Company, 2016.

Visit 12StoryLibrary.com

Scan the code or use your school's login at **12StoryLibrary.com** for recent updates about this topic and a full digital version of this book. Enjoy free access to:

- Digital ebook
- Breaking news updates
- Live content feeds
- Videos, interactive maps, and graphics
- Additional web resources

Note to educators: Visit 12StoryLibrary.com/register to sign up for free premium website access. Enjoy live content plus a full digital version of every 12-Story Library book you own for every student at your school.

Index

About the Author

Todd Kortemeier is a writer from Minneapolis, Minnesota. He is a graduate of the University of Minnesota's School of Journalism & Mass Communication. He has authored many books for young people.

READ MORE FROM 12-STORY LIBRARY

Every 12-Story Library book is available in many formats. For more information, visit 12StoryLibrary.com.